A Life of Two Halves

Nigel Fairweather

STOCKWELL
PUBLISHERS SINCE 1898

Published in 2022 by
NJF Books
Brixham, Devon
in association with
Arthur H Stockwell Ltd
West Wing Studios
Unit 166, The Mall
Luton, Bedfordshire
ahstockwell.co.uk

British Library Cataloguing-in-Publication Data:
A catalogue record for this book is
available from the British Library.
ISBN 9781526209283

Contents

This book is dedicated to my wife, Carol, who helped me with the manuscript, and to my late son, Mark; his twin brother, Andrew; my daughter, Teresa; and her sons, Leo and Walt.

A Life of Two Halves

Chapter One

Me and My Parents

My parents were John Henry Fairweather and Sybil Mary, neé Slade. My mother and her sisters, Joan and Margaret (Peggy), moved from Marlborough, Wiltshire, to Torquay, Devon, at the start of the Second World War (1939–1945). There Joan married Len Mudge, whom she had met at Catholic instruction classes, whilst Peggy remained single after an unfortunate encounter with an American serviceman.

My mother got a job as a receptionist at the Palm Court Hotel in Torquay. My father was a guest there, and I think they courted on the Rock Walk in Torquay and in the nearby village of Cockington. Another guest was the Scotsman John Logie Baird, who invented a mechanical type of television and the Baird Patent Sock – 'warm in the winter and cool in the summer'. Actually they were ordinary socks sprinkled with boracic powder! He would walk around the hotel lobby in his slippers – a typical absent-minded inventor.

Sybil and John were married at Sherford Church, a fourteenth-century building near Kingsbridge, Devon, which was built of local slate. They spent their wedding night at the Kings Arms Hotel in Kingsbridge – recently demolished. John was a farmer at Home Farm, East Charleton, also near Kingsbridge, with his brother, William Rossiter Fairweather (Ross), as his partner. They traded as Fairweather Brothers. Mum took a while to get used to living in a farmhouse with a slate floor in the kitchen and half-pigs hanging in the pantry.

I was born on 29 July 1943 at Home Farm – a vertex delivery aided by forceps applied by Dr Verniquet of Kingsbridge. I was eight pounds (whatever that is in metric), and Mum was so pleased with me that she took me up to the harvest field where my dad and the farmworkers were having their tea. This consisted of jam sandwiches (a double portion for Bill Putt, who was a big man with a voracious appetite) washed down with tea from a huge enamelled teapot which had been brought up from the farmhouse with a potato on its spout.

I was christened at Sherford Church and still have my (rather dog-eared) baptism certificate. The name Nigel came from a romantic novel Mum was reading at the time – a very English name. It was not long before Mum gave birth to Lorna Mary (her first name from Lorna Doone of Exmoor) and Heather (named after the purple flowers of Dartmoor).

When I was three years old, my dad became ill with Hodgkin's disease, also known as Hodgkin's lymphoma. This is a cancer of the lymphatic system and causes swellings in the armpits and neck. Mum was told there was no cure, even if she took him to Harley Street in London. Dad died in 1946, aged forty-three. I recently learned from a television programme that 'nitrogen mustard', used as a poison gas in the First World War, was used in the United States in 1940, and prolonged one patient's life by six months. This was the first anti-cancer drug, but it was kept secret and referred to as 'substance X'. These days a variety of anti-cancer drugs are used and a cure is possible.

In 1949, three years after John died, my mum married my father's brother, William Rossiter Fairweather (Ross). This had been made legal under an Act of Parliament between the wars. So our uncle became our stepfather. They went on to have a son, Graham Ross, and a daughter, Sybil Anne.

Lorna married John Fishlock and they ran a pub in Chippenham, then moved to Frogmore, near Kingsbridge. Now they live near Paphos, in Cyprus.

Heather married a Polish man called Jerzy (or George) and lived in South Brent. They had a daughter, Angela, and a son, Jason, but unfortunately Heather suffered from postnatal depression and took her own life.

Graham married an Irish Catholic girl called Noreen, who is a twin, ran the farm after Ross's death, and became an expert at DIY. He is now retired and lives in a barn at Home Farm, which he converted, called The Granary.

Both Ross and later Mum died of bowel cancer, Ross in his seventies and Mum at eighty-two.

Sybil Anne never married and, after suffering multiple fractures due to osteoporosis, moved from Home Farm (where she lived with Mum) to a nursing home at Totnes, where she is wheelchair-bound but seems contented.

Chapter Two

Schools

My father, John, went to Crediton Grammar School, Devon, and during the First World War he was very popular with his fellow pupils as he was able to obtain extra food from the farm where he lived (Malston, near Slapton, Devon). His brother, Ross, went to school at Kingsbridge, in what is now the Cookworthy Museum, and used to tie up the horse he rode from Malston at a relative's house. I do not know where Mum went to school, but she did get a medal for swimming, which is in my possession.

My first school was at Hazeldene, in Salcombe. I remember having a job to tie my shoelaces on my first day there. I was there from age five to eight, when boys had to leave, whilst girls carried on until they were about twelve. I recall doing maths on a trestle table outdoors, watching the girls playing tennis. We used to go down the hill to North Sands beach, and oddly I never noticed the drinking fountain there with an inscription including the name of James Fairweather, one of the Salcombe Fairweathers, of whom more later.

My next school was Montpelier, in Paignton, an all-boys prep school where we were taught Latin and Greek, geography, history, religious knowledge and French, but no science or modern history. The headmaster and his son-in-law, who taught us Latin, were martinets and I was caned twice. When I showed the scars on my buttocks to my sisters they gasped! (Later, at public school, I managed to get my Latin O level, but I was never any good at Greek.) We played cricket in our leisure time – mostly 'tip and run' – and rugby at other schools, sometimes in freezing weather. We had a Boy Scouts group, which I enjoyed, and I got several badges. There was a Natural History Club, where I specialised in astronomy(!), reading avidly about space exploration. Naturally I read all about Dan Dare, 'pilot of the future', in the *Eagle* comic. The headmaster refused permission for me to read the sister comic *Girl*, which my sisters could have passed on to me. We were allowed Arthur Mee's children's newspaper and my parents bought me a handsome set of the *Children's Cyclopedia*, also edited by him. Pop music was frowned on – I was not allowed to play a record of 'Singing the Blues' by Guy Mitchell – it was like Afghanistan under the Taliban! – but I did manage to listen to Radio Luxembourg after lights-out! We had the *Daily Telegraph* on weekdays (which supported our invasion of Suez), and *The Observer* on Sundays (which was against it), so we got a balanced view. On one occasion I organised a 'midnight feast' of chocolate bars, but we were caught and I was made to stay at school at weekends. What a swiz! I occupied the evenings making model planes out of balsa wood, little realising that one day I would fly with the Air Training Corps. I also made rugs with Reddicut wool, and wrote a newspaper called *The Reporter* in coloured inks. There was only one copy, but I passed it round. Ballpoint pens were forbidden, and we had inkwells and wood and metal pens or fountain pens. I sat my scholarship exams for Kingswood School, in Bath. I did well at maths and obtained a scholarship.

Kingswood was a Methodist school. It was founded in Kingswood, Bristol, but moved to the more salubrious city of Bath, Somerset. Instead of playing rugby in all weathers or doing 'public works' (sweeping up myriads of leaves in the school grounds), I was able to do photography, and became the treasurer of the photographic society. My job included making up developer from chemicals obtained from the chemistry lab. I can still remember the formula (Kodak D76, an 'MQ' developer): sodium carbonate 'of commerce', metol, quinol (another name for hydroquinone), and potassium metabisulphite as an antioxidant. In addition a layer of liquid paraffin was placed on top of the tank, also to prevent oxidation. Oxidised developer turns brown. Later I set up a darkroom at Home Farm, and did black-and-white processing, plus developing (and reversing by exposure to light) colour slide-film. In recent years I have returned to black-and-white developing and printing in a darkroom at my home in Brixham. More about that later.

Occasionally we would have a 'whole holiday' – a day off school when we could travel around by train, hitch-hiking or bicycling. A day with a good weather forecast was chosen, but if it turned to rain the whole holiday was cancelled and we had jam sandwiches (intended for the day out) fried in batter for lunch. By train I visited Bristol, where I got some illicit cigarettes from a machine, and Weston-super-Mare, where I bought a Jim Reeves LP. I went to Salisbury and photographed the cathedral, and one time cycled to Glastonbury. Unfortunately on the way back the top came off my headlight,

I braked sharply and went over the handlebars. I suffered a gash to my chin; but as it happened outside the fire station in Bath, a fireman kindly gave me a lift back to school. One day I visited the Long Ashton Agricultural Station, in Bristol, where Babycham was invented. It was marketed by Showerings of Shepton Mallet with the description 'The Genuine Champagne Perry' – i.e. sparkling pear juice. The champagne producers of France were not amused and eventually insisted that they stopped making that claim.

We had two services every Sunday and at one the famous Lord Soper preached. I joined the Air Training Corps and enjoyed a week with the RAF, including flying in dual-controlled Chipmunk planes.

The instructor, who sat in front of me, said, "I'll loop the loop and then you do one." (If you come out of the loop looking at the same straight rail line, for example, you are doing well.)

Then we did a barrel roll, after which I felt a bit queasy. I had to phone my mum and ask her to send me some travel-sickness tablets!

I got quite a lot of O levels, including the general paper, and even Latin! Then I opted for science A levels. After two years I passed physics, but failed chemistry. I was awarded an O level in biology on the strength of my A-level attempt. The biology classes included dissecting a dogfish and a rabbit. The fish had been preserved with smelly formalin, and the rabbit (which had been killed by putting it in a box with chloroform) became infested with maggots. I had to repeat a year at school and ended up with three A levels, including an S (scholarship) level in biology. I then had to choose between joining Ross on the farm and studying medicine. I was about to buy a pair of farm boots, when I was offered a place at Queen's College, Dundee, part of St Andrews University, to study medicine.

Chapter Three

University

Ten days later I went by train from Kingsbridge to London and took the sleeper to Glasgow Central Station. As I walked to Glasgow Queen Street Station I saw bridies, the Scottish version of Cornish pasties, in a shop window and bought one for my breakfast. Next I travelled alongside the River Tay to Dundee. The river is the subject of a poem by William McGonagall, said to be Scotland's worst poet, entitled 'Railway Bridge of the Silvery Tay':

> The Tay, the Tay, the Silvery Tay
> It flows past Dundee twice a day.

I spent one night in a hotel before moving into digs in Perth Road. I shared a room with Larry Levi, the son of a chemist from Chicago. His father sent him toothpaste and a large tin of ham, which he ate until the meat turned green! Larry and I bought a car between us, spending £40 on a 1938 Morris 8. The fuel gauge did not work and the driver's window was held up by string, but we managed to drive to Oban, on the west coast of Scotland, and back to Dundee without mishap. Eventually Larry went back to the USA and I sold the car for £10. At Queen's College I had a chance to brush up on my physics, chemistry and biology, and for chemistry I was top of the class and was awarded a bronze medal – no one got a gold or silver medal that year!

The next year I went into a hall of residence. One day I went down for breakfast in my dressing gown, which was against the rules – apparently it embarrassed the serving ladies. I was fined ten shillings, and as an unofficial punishment was dunked in a cold bath.

In the second year I studied physiology and anatomy, dissecting the body of some poor soul who was apparently a pauper. In one anatomy lecture the professor referred to the perineum as "an area of great surgical importance

– and I understand", he said, "that it is also of some social interest!" The next year we studied pathology and embryology; and although I struggled with both of these, I passed in the end.

When I was twenty-one my stepfather (Ross) bought me a Mini Countryman. When the car was delivered to Home Farm, the salesman from Oke Bros, in Kingsbridge, and Ross chatted over glasses of whisky. After a while Ross realised that the salesman wanted to be paid (£500). The Mini had been designed by Sir Alec Issigonis, who was born in Turkey. The 'east–west' engine was a novelty. Nowadays a transverse engine is used in many cars. My car was in Old English White with varnished wooden 'frames'. I used to sandpaper the wood and apply polyurethane yacht varnish. I drove this Mini from south Devon to Dundee, a distance of 600 miles, initially in one day, although later I would stop off with a dental-student friend near Stoke-on-Trent. The motorway network was incomplete at that time, and I had to drive through Wolverhampton on the way. On one journey smoke started to come from the exhaust, and I had to go to a garage in Preston, where the mechanic diagnosed a hole in a piston. I suppose I had driven the car very hard on motorways. I had to stay the night in a hotel and phone the Trustee Savings Bank in Dundee to obtain the money for an exchange engine. The next day I ran in the engine by driving to Dundee.

When it snowed (and I have known snow in June in Scotland) I went with a couple of girls to ski at Glenshee on several occasions. Once the car got stuck on an S-bend called the Devil's Elbow, near Glenshee, and I managed to persuade the girls to sit on the bonnet to improve traction because it was a front-wheel-drive car. One of them, N.L., was a chemistry student whom I dated for nearly a year. On one journey home I took her to her home in Sheffield and stayed the night there. Once the snow was so deep we could not reach the mountains, so we skied in some fields.

In my fifth year I shared a former rope-worker's cottage near Broughty Castle, just outside Dundee. One of my mates there was Akua Akan, the son of a paramount chief of the Ibo tribe in Nigeria, and also a medical student. He had a pre-war four-wheel-drive Morgan open sports car (the one we were to rebuild after we graduated). Akua and I travelled in my Mini to Glasgow one evening to see Marlene Dietrich singing at the Alhambra Theatre (she was being very coy about her age!). Driving through Glasgow on wet cobbles without the aid of a satnav was quite an experience, and so was the concert.

After the end of the summer term we had to wait about a month before we could graduate. Akua and I spent this time rebuilding his Morgan. He wanted to take it back to Nigeria, where he reckoned Ford parts would be easier to find than Morgan ones. We set off for various scrap-car dealers and acquired a Ford engine and gearbox, which were integral. (On the Morgan there was a short propshaft between the engine and the gearbox.) The originally blue car was repainted in Rootes Carnival Red. Later Akua did take it back to Nigeria, but he wrote it off going over a large pothole. He went on to become a surgeon and to run his own cement company. I saw him at a couple of 1968 medical-class reunions. By then he was working in Canada, and was kind enough to give me a paramount-chief outfit, which I have only worn once! Finally in 1968 Akua and I and our classmates graduated in a ceremony at the Caird Hall in Dundee. Caird was a jute-factory owner who also had a department store in Dundee. We duly put our hands up for the Hippocratic oath, which we did not take entirely seriously. '*Primum non nocere*' (Firstly do no harm) was fine, but promising never to procure an abortion had to be modified when the law changed. The graduation was supposed to be celebrated in the open air, but the heavens opened and there was thunder and lightning. Perhaps the Good Lord was not pleased with us! My mum and Aunty Peggy came to the graduation, travelling by Royal Blue coach to Victoria Coach Station in London, and then overnight on another coach to Edinburgh. I met them there and found that Mum's ankles were swollen after the journey. We went to a hotel in Princes Street and enjoyed a full Scottish breakfast, including smoked yellow haddock with a poached egg on top. We stayed at the new Angus Hotel in Dundee (since demolished for some reason). Whilst I was there I received a phone call from the hospital secretary at Freedom Fields Hospital, in Plymouth, where I had been appointed a junior house officer (JHO) in medicine. He asked if I could start two weeks early. I agreed, and launched on my medical career.

Chapter Four

Medicine

I was now a hospital doctor. One of my jobs was to take blood, nowadays done by a phlebotomist. The work was interesting, but tiring. I was on duty all night much of the time. One patient had haemophilia and I had to give him Factor VIII at 5 a.m. and 5 p.m. Since then we have learnt that such injections can lead to hepatitis or HIV.

I remember a private adult patient who had been admitted for a tonsillectomy. When I asked to take blood he said, "Can you wait until I have stopped shaving?"

After his operation he was given dispersible aspirin to gargle with and swallow. I was quite surprised, but this was insisted upon by the matron.

My senior house officer (SHO) was from Nepal – his brother was the Nepalese Ambassador to the United Nations. He came with me to visit Home Farm and gave me some gold cufflinks in the shape of a map of Nepal. Another young man died in the ward from asthma. These days I don't think this would happen, thanks to steroid inhalers and Salbutamol inhalations.

For one holiday I drove all the way to the Isle of Skye, but the island was actually pretty boring. I went on to a hotel in Aviemore – a skiing centre. I did not ski, but went on the ice rink. Then I went back to my student city of Dundee.

For my next holiday the Nepalese doctor and I visited as many countries in Europe as we could manage in a fortnight, travelling in my Mini. The Channel Tunnel had not yet been opened, and we crossed by ferry. From Calais we went to Waterloo, near Brussels, in Belgium. The landlady must have thought my companion was female, as she gave us a double bed! Also, there was no supper – just a bottle of beer each. We went on through Luxembourg to France and then Switzerland. At Zurich I asked a young lady the way to our hotel. She said she did not know, but her price for the night was fifty Swiss francs. I politely declined. We continued through Liechtenstein (blink and you miss it) and then on to a hotel on the beautiful Lake Wolfgangsee, in Austria, where we stayed for three days. Next we went via the spa town of Baden-Baden to Amsterdam, where a lady driver in a Daf bumped into the rear of my car when I stopped at tramlines.

A female policeman came along and said in English, "A woman driver – obviously her fault. Go back to England and don't worry about it."

When I got home I repaired the damaged woodwork with Plastic Wood and varnish and fitted a new winker unit.

My next job was as a JHO in surgery at Greenbank Hospital, near Freedom Fields Hospital. Later both hospitals, and the Royal Naval Hospital at Devonport, were combined to form Derriford Hospital on the outskirts of Plymouth. The surgical job was just as tiring as the medical one, but I discovered a good wheeze. At around 6 p.m., when I was due to be on call all night, I would ring the JHO at the Royal Naval Hospital and say that my ward was full, and ask him to take calls for the rest of the night. This worked OK until I was nearly at the end of my six-month job, when a very senior officer at the naval hospital rang to see what I had been up to! This didn't worry me, as I was finishing the job soon.

Whilst I was at Greenbank I met a sister from the children's ward at a party. I ended up proposing to her, and when I visited her mother in Cornwall I was greeted with a saffron cake – a traditional Cornish recipe. Saffron is a yellow spice made from the stigma and styles of crocus flowers, and is, weight for weight, more expensive than gold. (Many years later my wife, Carol, and I were to make saffron cake ourselves.) The engagement fell through after I didn't succeed in getting a post as a SHO in obstetrics and gynaecology at the North Devon Infirmary in Barnstaple.

Instead I applied for a similar job at St Margaret's Hospital in Epping, Essex. Unfortunately I did not realise how long it would take to get from Central London to Epping on the Underground train and was late for the interview. I was offered a job in obstetrics and gynaecology provided I did six months in geriatrics first. I accepted, but did not enjoy geriatrics much. Obstetrics and gynaecology was more interesting. The hospital had been built to house patients from the London Hospital during the Second World War, as it was feared the London Hospital would be bombed. The wards were rather basic huts, but a new accident-and-emergency unit had been added – always called casualty. One day a Belgian woman arrived at casualty asking for an abortion, as that was not legal in her own country. She was referred to me and I took advice from my registrar, as abortions were not yet legal here; I don't know what happened after that.

During my time in Epping I used to go with a male radiographer friend to the Star of India Restaurant in Walthamstow, where we had very hot curries with onion bhajis. I also went with him to see the film *Dr Zhivago*, which we enjoyed even though we arrived late. For a holiday break I went on a sailing course at the Island Cruising Club in Salcombe. I stayed on their boat, which was moored in 'The Bag' – the name for Salcombe Estuary, which resembles an upside-down cow's udder. One day I went to an interview at Torbay Hospital and it was agreed that I could take up the post of SHO in paediatrics. I missed a day's tuition in knots, but the club kindly turned a blind eye and gave me a Yachting Certificate anyway!

At Torbay Hospital I worked on the children's ward and also covered for a colleague in obstetrics and gynaecology on alternate nights and weekends. On one memorable occasion I was called to the Accident and Emergency Department to see a child with quinsy – a severe inflammation of the throat. I got the anaesthetic registrar to come to my aid. Another child was admitted after swallowing some Weedol (paraquat) weedkiller. I looked up the treatment, and it was oral bentonite kaolin, which the pharmacy was able to supply. The child recovered, but it was not until I was writing this book that I discovered what bentonite is. It is, in fact, a kind of absorbent clay formed by a breakdown of volcanic ash, and it is named after Fort Benton in Montana, USA, where it is found.

Whilst I was working at Torbay Hospital I became engaged to a Miss Y, who was a staff nurse on permanent night duty. She used to make me Ovaltine or Horlicks when I visited the ward at night. We watched *Poldark* and *The Onedin Line* at her house in Paignton, where she lived with her sister and father. Sadly, her mother had died after an operation at the hospital. The family had previously lived in Kenya, where her father was a tobacco agent. She wanted me to get a post as a GP in the Torbay area, starting as a trainee. I applied to every practice in the area, but had no luck. Eventually we decided to part, and I went on to become a trainee GP at a health centre in Exeter.

My trainer was kind enough to find me a flat in a development called Lansdowne. It was a co-ownership flat, and if you stayed there for forty years it was yours. In fact I stayed for one year. I cooked for myself – for example, I would make a bread-and-butter pudding and save half for the next day. My most memorable case was that of an unmarried mother at a Catholic maternity home. I went with my trainer, and he left me to conduct the delivery with the help of a nun-midwife. They didn't have any rubber gloves, and neither did I, so I used my bare hands. Whilst putting in a local anaesthetic so that an incision called an episiotomy could be made to ease the delivery, I poked my finger with the needle. However, no harm was done to me or the young mother. Sadly the baby was taken from her for adoption. I hope this sort of thing does not happen these days.

Whilst at Lansdowne I was visited by a Miss W, who lived in the same block of flats. She was a health visitor, who complained that the doctors at her health centre did not believe in health visitors and did not give her enough work to do. We dated on and off for several years, and on one occasion she took me in her Daf car (with its unique automatic transmission by a rubber belt) to Barnstaple, where she had become a school counsellor and violin teacher. I sat in her class whilst she gave a violin lesson. As she was quite a lot older than me, I assumed (she never told me her age!), I was not too sure about marriage, and for my next job I went back to Dundee to become an SHO in the Accident & Emergency Department. At about 6 a.m. one morning, when I was on night shift, a man was brought in whose head had been trapped between buffers on the railway. One pinna (the flap of the ear) had been severed, and I sent him for an X-ray to exclude a fractured skull. Later he was admitted to the Plastic Surgery Ward, and the doctor there told me off for not sending him straight to them to have his ear stitched back on. You live and learn!

Sir Edmund Hillary, who with Tenzing Norgay was the first to climb Mount Everest, came in after injuring a leg on a Scottish hillside. The casualty consultant came to the unit to treat him!

On one day off I went down to the harbour and got on board a sailing ship. Here I copied with pencil a painting of a ship which was on display. I am no artist (except for photography!), but I can copy things.

After that I did various GP and hospital-locum jobs. In Taunton I worked in a practice where I was given lunch each day. There was cold tongue every day for a week! Eventually I got a post as an SHO at Falmouth Hospital, alongside an Indian doctor called Anugen Bhatt. We took turns in covering the wards and minor operations. Although Truro is the county town of Cornwall, Falmouth has a bigger population. On the gynaecology ward, a nurse reported that a patient seemed confused. I explained to her that when someone seems confused they might in fact be in pain.

"I'll teach the nurses," said the ward sister.

Oh dear!

In the casualty unit I used to explain to people how their accident could have been prevented. The sister didn't like this one little bit. The nurses used to ask patients to 'lay' on the examination couch. I looked this up in a dictionary, as I thought they should say 'lie'. It said the use of 'lay' was archaic or nautical. Again, the sister did not like it. Nevertheless I enjoyed my time in 'minor ops'.

When a patient was X-rayed I would often go and ask the radiographer's opinion as to whether there was a fracture. The radiographers were based at the old City Hospital in Truro, and took turns to come to Falmouth. One radiographer called Carol caught my eye, and after lunch in the staff canteen one day I asked her if she was married.

"No" came the reply, and I was hooked!

We were soon engaged and were married on 30 October 1976 at Newquay Wesley Church. We spent our first night together at a hotel in Plymouth, and the next day we took the ferry to Roscoff in Brittany, France. I told the taxi driver who took us from the port to our hotel that "Nous sommes en notre voyage de noces," and he cheekily replied, "Faites l'amour comme les chiens"! We enjoyed our honeymoon driving around Brittany, and then I resumed work as a salaried partner in general practice in an Essex town.

Chapter Five

General Practice

A man came to see me about enlargement of his breasts. It turned out that he had been given stilboestrol, a female hormone, instead of salbutamol for his asthma. Hard-to-read writing on his repeat prescription card had led to the receptionist writing out a prescription for the hormone. (Many years later I developed tender breast enlargement due to the psychotropic drug olanzepine acting as a pseudo-hormone.)

My next post was in Lincolnshire. The doctors were members of an emergency team for road traffic accidents, and we had a radio on which we could receive messages, with another radio being used by our wives. I also used the radio to ask Carol if there were any more calls after a visit to a patient of a practice about fifteen miles away, with which we shared a weekend rota. On the way back from a visit in that area, I radioed my wife to say that I was nearly home but stuck behind a herd of cows. (She was breastfeeding Teresa at the time.) Another doctor who had a radio on the same frequency complained that I was misusing the radio. So much for co-operation!

I found that quite a few X-ray results were filed in the wrong notes, and I took it upon myself to write to the consultant radiologist at the local hospital to suggest better ways of identifying the patients. The partners who employed me were not at all pleased with this, as I had not discussed it with them. One morning I was asked to visit a patient whose appendix scar had burst, and I suggested that a district nurse could visit him and if necessary admit him to hospital. This didn't go down well!

I visited a patient who was on a diuretic tablet called frusemide (now renamed furosemide), together with four tablets of potassium called Slow-K per day. He was complaining of upper-abdominal pain and I thought this was stomach irritation due to the Slow-K. I therefore changed his tablets to Frumil (Co-amilofruse), which contains frusemide and the potassium-conserving diuretic amiloride. Apparently the partner who had put him on Slow-K was not impressed. These days it is not felt essential to give potassium or amiloride with furosemide. So for a variety of reasons I left the practice and was lucky enough to obtain a position as a full partner in Northamptonshire.

Whilst I was in this practice there were several memorable events. One elderly lady told me she had trouble with her 'wagina'. Actually the Romans did pronounce V as W, as in *Veni, vidi, vici* – I came, I saw, I conquered. In fact she simply had candidiasis or thrush, a common fungal infection. The proprietor of a nursing home gave me gifts, including a model of the Taj Mahal which eventually deliquesced away – i.e. became liquid by absorbing moisture from the air. She used to give me coffee and cakes like rum baba, which I am very fond of. She invited me to come over one evening for a curry, but whilst I was eating it I found that she was spiking my orange juice with vodka. Perhaps she fancied me!

Another patient on whom I had done a rectal examination at home (without a chaperone) to exclude appendicitis came to my surgery later and announced, "You must realise my feelings for you by now, Doctor!" She was a violin tutor to the son of one of my partners. I fled to the office!

I was called to see a man who had been found dead in his bedroom. He had a dent in his skull and I assumed that he had fallen and hit his head on the wardrobe. Within a few days the police told me that he was a homosexual and had been hit on the head with a blunt instrument. They took a statement from me and took my fingerprints, by asking me to roll tins on the table. They also tried to place my accent, and concluded that it was Oxford English – i.e. received pronunciation!

One middle-aged lady came to see me about feeling tired. I arranged thyroid-function tests which showed she was hypothyroid – so she went on to take levothyroxine tablets for life. I enjoyed this sort of detective work.

Chapter Six

1086 and All That

Whilst I was a GP in Northamptonshire I enrolled with the Open University. After unsuccessful attempts in English literature and French, I opted for courses in family and local history, and English 'from Chaucer to the Internet'. It was the last year they offered family and local history, so I grabbed my chance as family history was already a hobby of mine. I first became interested in this when my stepfather, Ross, received a letter from a firm of solicitors in Bristol – they were trying to trace relatives of a lady who had died intestate. They wanted to know if Ross was related to a John Fairweather who lived in the nineteenth century. I was never able to answer that question with certainty as a great many of my ancestors were called John Fairweather – a traditional name for the firstborn son.

One day, the last day of October and the last day of the season when the Salcombe Maritime Museum was open, Carol and I visited it and found a wallchart of the family history of a Len Fairweather who was 'the last of the Salcombe Fairweathers'. The chart had been drawn up by a Mr Murch, who was a designer of ships and a maker of model boats. He had acquired the family-history papers of Len after he had died. They were stored in a garage and his widow was about to destroy them. The chart showed the marriage of John Fairweather to Agnes Redwarde in 1571 at Malborough Church. Until about 1840 Salcombe did not have a church. It only had a chapel as it was a small fishing village, so births, marriages and deaths were recorded by the parish priest at nearby Malborough. Henry VIII had first instructed priests to keep a record of births, marriages and deaths on paper. His daughter Elizabeth I decreed that these should be transcribed by the priests on to parchment (the skin of sheep or goats), which would be more permanent. (To this day, Acts of Parliament are stored on rolls of parchment in the House of Lords.)

Alongside the family tree were photos taken by James Fairweather of ships in Salcombe Harbour. James was a newspaper editor (the *Salcombe Gazette*), a Justice of the Peace and chairman of Salcombe Urban District Council. He is commemorated on a drinking fountain at North Sands, Salcombe. The name of the town was cut out at the time of the Second World War so any German troops landing would not know where they were. It was reinstated after the war. Armed with this chart, and the 1814 diary of Jarvis Fairweather plus a family Bible kept from about 1850 to 1950 I was able to construct my family tree.

Jarvis wrote the details of his life in 1814 in a diary published in Exeter, which was passed down to me. He describes the death of his first wife ten days after a stillbirth – no doubt due to puerperal sepsis consequent on being delivered by a surgeon who visited for the birth and aftercare, but carried infection on his hands. This was before the Hungarian obstetrician Ignaz Semmelweis insisted on sterile precautions during a delivery. Jarvis married again and a daughter from that marriage lived to be 100. Her married name was Honeywell, and a descendant lived at Beeson, South Devon – I have met her.

Jarvis lived at Lower Coltscombe, near Slapton, but the earlier Fairweathers lived at Horsecombe, near Batson, just outside Salcombe. In the Domesday Book (1086) it was called Hornercombe, and the book lists the numbers of villeins (farmworkers), sheep and cattle, together with the 'rateable value' under the ancien régime of King Harold, who died at the Battle of Hastings in 1066.

Close to Horsecombe is a derelict house called La Vierge (The Virgin). When I explored it I found that there was a shelf in the corner of a room decorated with red and white roses, from the Wars of the Roses. The stairs were in a bad state of repair, so I didn't go upstairs. In the garden stood a slate with a nick in the side 'for tightening your crossbow'.

For my Bachelor of Arts degree I undertook some research. I compared the celebrations for Queen Victoria's gold and diamond jubilees in the local paper (the *Kingsbridge Gazette*), which I accessed on microfilm at the Cookworthy Museum, in Kingsbridge. The celebrations, with bunting, etc., seemed much the same, though the Queen had become rather unpopular in her widowhood.

For my second piece of research I decided to use the possession of resident servants as a measure of being middle class. I studied the census returns of 1881 for the St David's area of Exeter (near the railway station) and Lower Brixham, also known locally as Fishtown. It turned out that the

Exeter households had more resident servants, whereas the inhabitants of Fishtown, mostly fishermen's families, were less likely to have them. For another research project, Carol and I looked at the MOH (Medical Officer of Health) annual reports from about 1860 to 1960, when the post of MOH was abolished. We saw these reports in the Local History section of Exeter Library. They were printed except for those for the Second World War, which were typed. We noted the infant mortality rate (number of deaths in the first year per 1,000 live births) for Okehampton Rural District. The IMR came down from about fourteen to four over the century. This was largely due to the reduction in deaths from such diseases as measles and diphtheria, and purer water supplies. The IMR is widely regarded as a measure of the health of a community.

Chapter Seven

Photographer

At prep school I had a very simple 828 camera, which produced tiny prints. Later I used my mother's 1920 Kodak folding 'Autographic' camera, which was made in Canada and took 120 films. Initially 'Autographic' films were available on which details of each print could be recorded with a stylus. By the time I used the camera, only ordinary 120 film was available. I used to take flash photographs by using the 'B' (bulb) setting, opening the shutter of the camera, firing a flash, and then closing the shutter again. Needless to say this was all in black-and-white. Then my Uncle Ron (my mother's brother, who worked in intelligence during the war and then became deputy editor of Hansard in the House of Commons) gave me a 127 Brownie camera. I soon branched out into colour film, and later my parents bought me an Agfa Silette 35-mm camera, which was very basic but gave good results. I photographed the wedding of my cousin Janet (Uncle Ron's daughter) to Mike Rushby on Ferraniacolor, and the next day developed the pictures myself. The same day I was able to show the slides to Uncle Ron and his wife Gwen, and Janet and Mike received Kodacolor duplicates.

When I retired as a GP, at the age of fifty-four, I worked in a Jessops photographic store for a while, and the deputy manager passed on to me a copy of the programme for a Fujifilm wedding-photography course at Cheltenham Art College. I jumped at this opportunity, and after the course I resolved to begin a second career as a wedding photographer. We moved to Brixham because I had always wanted to live in Devon, and because my son Mark wished to study art at South Devon College in Torquay, which was served by buses from Brixham.

Soon after I started photographing weddings I took on a friend called Rachel, who was six years older than me, as an assistant. She helped to organise the groups at weddings. Before I took her on I had photographed the wedding of a nursing sister, and her grandma was not visible in the big group photo! She complained, but didn't ask for any refund. I learned my lesson. I went on to receive complimentary remarks about most of my wedding pictures, though one couple complained that an enlargement was too grainy.

For weddings I used a Minolta 7000 single-lens reflex 35-mm camera and a Mamiya 645 single-lens reflex camera, which took sixteen pictures on 120 film. I used Kodak Portra and the equivalent Fuji professional films, which gave true skin colours rather than the bright colours of amateur films. One couple asked for their photos to be taken by candlelight, and I did so using twelve candles in two candelabras and free samples of an experimental 800 ASA Fujicolor film, which was twice as fast as their usual fast colour film. I enjoyed photographing weddings, but never made a profit because I didn't charge enough to cover the cost of taking about 100 photos and getting them printed at a professional lab. The couples received forty pictures in a preview album, and they chose from there twenty pictures to go in a white Spicer Hallfield album with tissue between each page, just like Carol and I had for our wedding. The most popular size was 5" × 7". Examples of my wedding photos and of other pictures taken on an A-level course at South Devon College are included in this book, together with some other pictures which I am proud of.

Chapter Eight

Children

Our daughter Teresa (born in 1977), attended a Quaker school called Sibford, near Banbury, Oxfordshire, and went on to get a first in chemistry from the University of Nottingham. She travelled to Nepal and then to India, where she met Evan Walker, an Australian. Carol and I flew to Melbourne and I photographed their wedding at the Women's Centre, formerly the Victoria Women's Hospital. They separated after they could not agree on their future plans. Teresa met Glenn Jones when they were both working as chemists, and they had two boys, Leo and Walt. They got married on a beach. They now live inland from Brisbane, out in the country, and we have visited them several times, usually flying via Singapore, Kuala Lumpur or Dubai.

Fifteen months after Teresa Claire was born, Carol had non-identical twins, Andrew John and Mark Ross. She had presumably released an egg from each ovum simultaneously. Mark was a small baby and choked on his milk. A barium swallow at Kettering showed a tracheo-oesophageal fistula (TOF) and oesophageal atresia. He had an operation for this at the old Radcliffe Infirmary at Oxford when one day old. I took some of the breast milk which Carol had expressed in frozen form to Oxford. Like Teresa, the boys went to local state schools, and later Sibford School, and afterwards they attended local art colleges. They both went on to university to study art – Andrew to Huddersfield and Mark to the North Wales School of Art at Glyndwr University, in Wrexham.

On 30 July 2020 Mark choked on a piece of steak and could not be saved, despite the efforts of first-aiders and paramedics. He was forty-one years old. On several occasions during his life he had choked on food, as the operation had left him with a section of his oesophagus which did not propel food downwards normally. We were all very sad when Mark died, and we gave him a proper funeral which included two of his favourite songs, 'Walking in the Air', from *The Snowman*, and 'You'll Never Walk Alone'. Mark is buried in the Woodland Cemetery at Torquay and his memorial plaque says, 'We loved him'.

Chapter Nine

The Twenty-First Century

In 2017 my mobility worsened. I was found to have Parkinson's Disease and ended up in a wheelchair. However, thanks to some clever capsules called Madopar I am 99% better and am simply left with occasional tremor of my left hand.

In 2019 I started to get angina at night and was admitted to Torbay Hospital, where it was found that I had suffered a heart attack. A coronary angiogram showed blockage of two of my coronary arteries and I was transferred to Derriford Hospital in Plymouth where I had a so-called *CABBAGE* operation – Coronary Artery By-Pass Grafts x2. I made a good recovery.

***

The biggest event of the twenty-first century has been the coronavirus, also known as Covid-19, which I shall call simply Covid. As you will know, the first occurrence of a new type of respiratory viral pneumonia occurred in Wuhan in China in November 2019. It soon spread around the world and so was called a pandemic. In the UK we went into our first lockdown in March 2020, and our second one in October. In December it was announced that approval had been given for the use of the Pfizer-BioNTec vaccine, and soon afterwards the AstraZeneca vaccine was approved. As I was over seventy and 'extremely vulnerable' because of previous heart surgery in 2019 and Parkinsonism I was given a jab in January 2021 and Carol was allowed to have one at the same time. We had our second vaccinations in April and gave a sigh of relief. Meantime my niece Angela and her three children, who live in Milton Keynes, tested positive for Covid, but none of them needed to go into hospital. We have subsequently met up with them and they are back to normal.

At the time of writing (August 2021) I am glad to say that most restrictions were ended last month, and from later this month the need for contacts of those who test positive for Covid to self-isolate will be abolished in England.

We spent an interesting forties weekend at the Severn Valley Railway last month. This included a musical evening with jitterbug dancing on the Saturday and a ride on a steam train from Kidderminster to Bridgnorth on the Sunday (one of the photos is printed in this book). I was particularly pleased with a picture of me as a sailor grabbing Carol as a Red Cross nurse for a kiss, reminiscent of the famous picture taken in New York on VJ day in 1945. Covid precautions were taken throughout the weekend, and I bought a cotton mask with a picture of jitterbugging on it! This autumn we hope to go to Yorkshire for a holiday, and maybe in a year or two we will be able to join Teresa and her family, flying via Los Angeles for a tour of New Zealand and then going on to Australia. Who knows what the future holds?

Thank you for buying this book. Writing it has been very therapeutic for me in these difficult times.

Postscript: Since I wrote this chapter, the news is all about Afghanistan and whether strict sharia law will be introduced. As I said before, it sounds rather like my prep school!

PPS: Since I typed this book Ukraine is the main news item. I campaign against the war, and work as a volunteer in a church café and enjoy attending art classes – a new interest for me.

Henry Fairweather, my paternal grandfather.

My parents John Henry Fairweather and Sybil Mary (neé Slade), the only surviving wedding photo.

Me in the arms of my mother Sybil Mary Fairweather (neé Slade) at Home Farm.

My uncle and step-father,
William Rossiter Fairweather ('Ross').

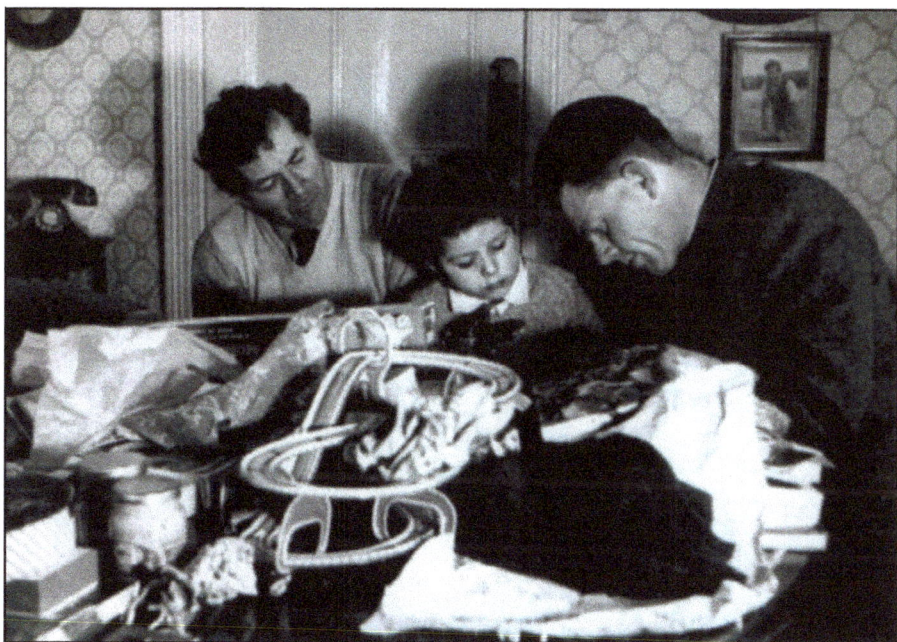

Ross, Graham and my cousin, Philip Gubbin at Home Farm.

The author in a tree.

The author at Frogmore Creek.

The author and Carol Margaret (neé Woodcock), cutting our wedding cake.

Carol at the National Maritime Museum, Falmouth.

Our twin boys, Andrew John and Mark Ross (not identical).

Walt and Leo, our grandsons.

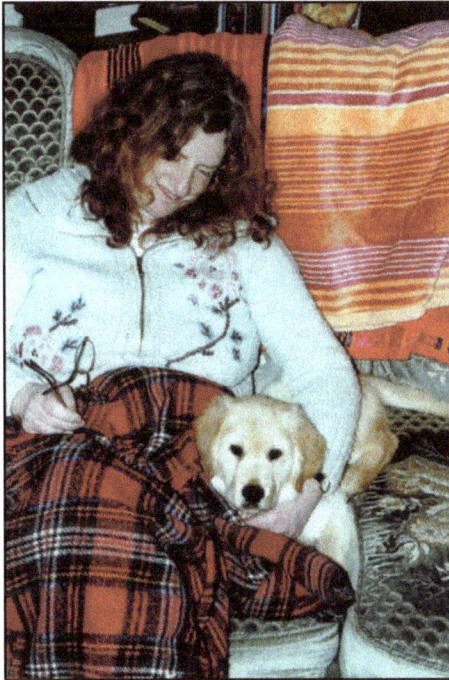

Carol with our second Golden Retriever, Toby.

Our daughter Teresa Claire with her husband, Glenn Jones and their dogs at their home in Australia.

Leo and Walt, our grandchildren, with toy dinosaurs knitted by Carol.

Carol at Broadsands beach, Paignton.

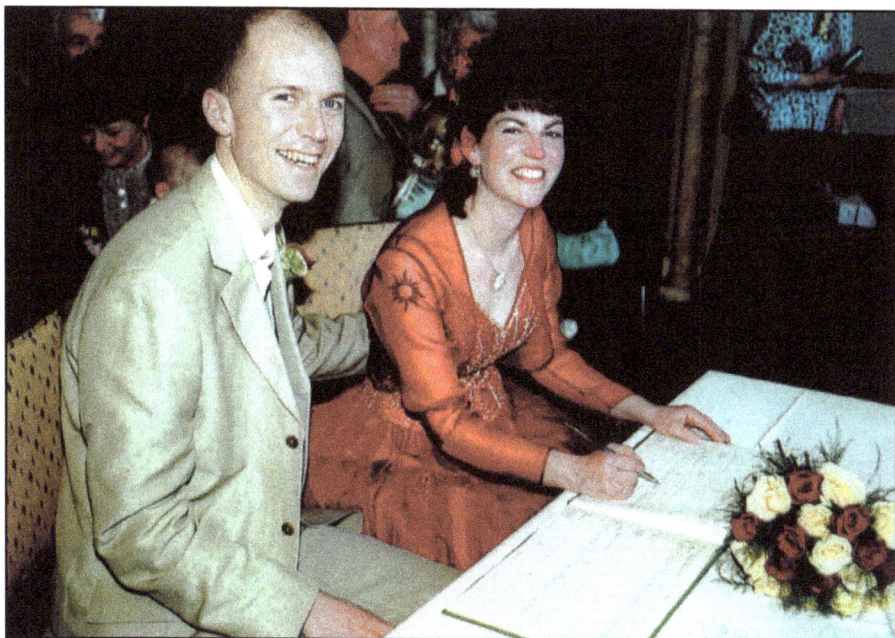

Steve Sayers and Joanna (neé Woodcock) signing the marriage register.

Carol and the author on a forties weekend on the Severn Valley Railway.

Swan.

'The Birth of Venus' by Botticelli. Acrylic painting by numbers.

Model number one.

Model number two.

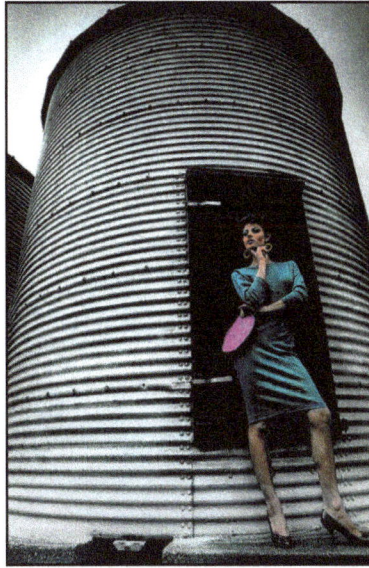

Model number three. Hand coloured with inks.

Model number four, a fellow student on
A-level photography course, South Devon College.

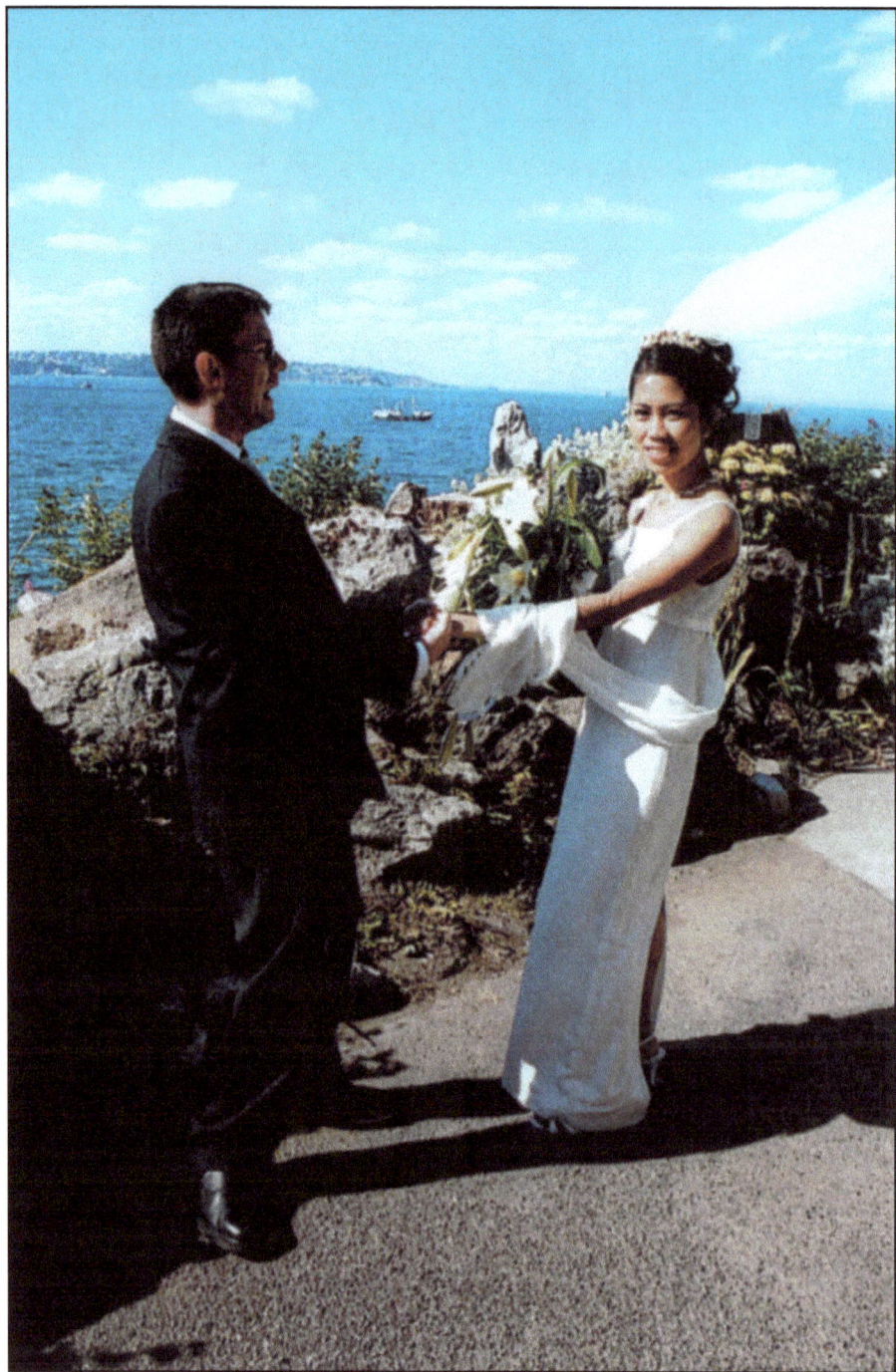

A wedding at the Berry Head Hotel, Brixham.

A wedding photographed by candlelight.

A draft advertisement featuring a model car.

The 'Man and Boy' sculpture in Brixham.